Our Diminishments

# Our Diminishments

## Poems by

### Robin Amelia Morris

Cover design by Shay Culligan:

ISBN: 978-1-950462-91-9

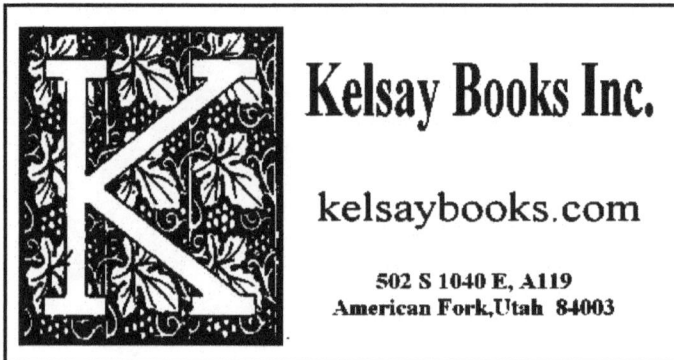

# Kelsay Books Inc.

kelsaybooks.com

**502 S 1040 E, A119
American Fork, Utah 84003**

# Acknowledgments

Many thanks to the editors of the following journals in which these poems, some in different format, first appeared.

*American Literary Review:* "1984 and Counting"

*The Lowell Review:* "Gravity Stoop"

*Lilith:* "My Destiny"

*Bakunin:* "Oscillations"

*Salt River Review:* "Smut Creek"

*Comstock Review:* "Sticky Truth"

*North American Review:* "Towering Graveyard"

*San Pedro River Review:* "Vagabond on the Fourth of July"

# Contents

# Welcome

Child, old and heavy
with knowledge that began
the day you were thrust
into this world: listen.

A branch is tearing itself
from its tree. Flinging itself
onto forest floor. Jays squawk displeasure
like wives on the hurricane news
holding up boards and bricks to patch
the emptiness opening up everywhere.

Meanwhile, on my block, a house grows
on a wooden frame. The one I live in is for sale.
All that remains of its earlier inhabitants:
a series of notches on a door lintel
marking the height of someone who stopped
in '87 or moved away.

If I could amass all the data on these trees,
I would warn birds to secure
their precarious nests. I'd sing
like wind. But there is no wind.
The ground with its litter
of leaves registers no response

to the newly fallen limb.
This is the welcome
you have yet to fathom.

# The Forgetting

If you ask where I have been
my worn tires will not squeal.
Unpaving itself, the road
remembers only sand.

I will answer once. I will speak
of a sky that conceals rocks
and of a baby, fooled by soft coups,
spitting up the Latin names of plants.

Bursting with tiny selves, I run
to the last candy store
where, since the dusty blast,
the proprietor sells nothing

but green glass bottles
and asks me to breathe water.
Suddenly he is a salamander.
The rocks are heavy and red.

# Sour Oats

As a child, nothing stood in my way
but the world. I knew a wise Arabian
horse was grazing somewhere in my future
and I'd ride him out of the neighborhood,

creating a stir on those asphalt fields—
Red Road and Grange, acoustically designed
so my mother's howl could always find me.
Now the horse is nuzzling the crank

on my hospital bed: unwinding.
He steps back into rock gardens
and swing sets, splashes through blue pools,
unsaddled, never ridden.

# In or Out

They matched in a way.
    Aqua blue and green ferns
    coiling on vinyl tablecloth
    echoed green and blue sheaves of wheat
    on cracked wallpaper above.
The phone was beige.
    Mother held it to her ear:
    "uh-huh, uh-huh" (hand
    over mouthpiece): "shhh!
    "Go outside and play.
    "uh-huh, I see."
Carrying my bucket of chalk,
    I skipped out past piles of newspapers,
    cat food dishes licked clean,
    ants looking for remains,
    to the driveway where
I began to draw. Mansions, cabins, mock
    Tudor colonials. Exotic exteriors
    perfect until the next rain.

# Aubade with Cat Lady

My mother's breakfast call penetrates the block,
ringing through toothbrushes, coffee cups,

shaking loose a stir in shrubbery as whiskers emerge.
Noses sniff air laden with bacon and Dial soap.

"Here kitty kitty kitty," the high note resounds, bounces
off stucco and brick, slips through Venetian blinds, slinking

like the felines checking for scent of rivals
on leaf and chair leg, ignoring the hedgehog

who lives below the porch sagging with bundled newspapers.
They strop her pajama'd legs and offer up purrs.

# Gravity Stoop

I want to stop them because I know
what the result will be; but while they're falling,
the leaves articulate space
between trees, singing, "here's light,"
and "here" and "here."

Earth's core pulls harder in some places
and things that should take wing cannot,
but instead, sink deep into themselves.
My grandmother's front stoop was such a place,
where compass needles, unable to detect north,
spun recklessly. My parents could never forgive
Grandma for opening her arms: I fell upon the stoop.
Baby teeth spilled on brick and when they grew out
one bore the Hebrew letter *hey,* a cloud,
white on white enamel,
shaped like the moon in eclipse,
a bowl turned over
to spill its fresh cream onto earth.

All those autumns that have happened since,
each year a new notebook, the string section swelling,
and all the time I'm forgetting the stoop
and squinting at people like they're crazy when they ask.
I try out Cain's old line: "what mark?" and it works.

# Kitchen Magician

The linoleum is shriveling,
opening a space below the door
through which a herd

of tiny telephones sails.
Oh my kitchen, my dirty
radicchio riddled realm,

my make peace wail, my
tomorrow I'll scrub you
till clean is a lesson

in graphic exploitation.
Temper tantrums squall in
and out of cupboards.

In this cracked cloister
hummingbirds sip silence
from a freezer door

which won't make ice.
Here a drug of nesting
tucks me into a corner.

I have always been here,
will always, while my roots
rot in chemical sod,

the love canal through which I entered
and headed toward a future
made possible by oxygen tanks

even a toddler can fix,
the will to survive just balancing
its opposite urge.

# 1984 and Counting

My eyelashes, like crow's wings
flapping on the inner pane of my glasses...

Focus shifts and there's the stubbed out
cigarette in the Lago di Como ashtray,

someone else's souvenir that I purchased
from a Thrift Shop. Thrifty, you could say

that describes me at moments. Someone who always
resumes the last point after being interrupted,

who's planning to continue that conversation
with herself she left off sometime in the Eighties.

A rough decade, not only because
the prophetic book title brooded over it

but I had my reasons, I suppose, for subjecting
myself to tyrants, donning hair shirts and garter belts,

getting myself into the primal pose
with the man from Opus Dei

right in his backyard where the neighbors could see
so I had to spend some of the decade hiding in a cage.

Where was I? Oh yes, my lashes, flapping
like a crow. But it's really not my thoughts,

it's these, rising from the page, that draw
the attention through their reedy eye

then let it go in a gentle exhale.
My sight flickers, in and out.

What is this insistent unweaving
but some assignment I took on before my birth?

For this the defenders of the preborn
laid siege to the primal gateway and granted me passage

to a world of Spin-Art, roses, and cancelled elections.
I am greeted each morning by twenty seven doormen

who all know my name and social security number.
The elevator buttons have been replaced

by a flashing spiral that replicates
the location of my cell from which I can foresee

no further interruptions, nothing to distract me
from the impossible task of remembering.

# Oscillations

More and more frequently, the music's
cut off, mid-note; its sudden decay
hanging out over the edge of silence.

This lasts for a second or two and then
the emergency broadcast signal takes over.
Any attempt to get more out of Beethoven

becomes futile and I find myself
humming along with the tone, praying
with its wire melody for attention.

We will receive instruction.
But only in an actual emergency.

I thought mine was.
But considering the disaster this radio warning
promises, I register only a patient fire.

No figure like a smooth Egyptian feline
with infinite space whizzing behind its glass face
waits at my mirror.

If I were in another mood I'd tell you
in succinct syllables that evoke each crack
of my eye swirling and content as a lava bed—

But see, I'm a slave to triumph, remorse, rage,
apathy. My smile floats back, a message
sent by my once serotonin-filled brain,

like a note magnetized to the refrigerator:
*I'll be home soon.*

The signal beats a smooth sixty cycles.
Sine waves, carriers of purest sound,
caught up in the moment before silence returns,

before I begin to chant, *I'm here, I'm here.*

# Room Tone

Silence has a shape
Chisels corners

Clings to sparest wall
Sinks into carpet

The sharp listener can tell
Where each silence was born

What space it describes
With invisible hands

Affectionate hum
Deep in the belly of dimension

Making sure we never hear
The shape true silence takes

# My Destiny

My Ancestors have put on weight,
their bodies white against the skyline
of Brooklyn or Warsaw,
bath slippers skimming over black roof.

They tan but do not age,
saying, "the sky was never like this.
So uncluttered, so gay." I come up
once a week with Coppertone and the Sunday

Times. It's enough, it takes them all week
to argue through seventeen sections.
When I tell them I'm expecting, they nod
and their heads bow

like sunflowers heavy with wisdom, dropping seeds.
They suggest names: "after Uncle Able.
If he hadn't pulled me off the picket line
to meet your grandfather..."

Months later, my belly still flat as a puddle,
they throw me a shower, the only rain
since the first sleepless night I climbed
those rusty stairs to look down at courtyards

that shriek with streetlight.
I give birth. They stand around as my head
emerges from between my own legs, grinning
and spitting tailor's chalk, pins.

Up on tar beach, this so called fire-escape
where rescue can only come from above,
there's nothing to do but study the geography
of my recent mistakes.

Municipal shrubs pruned into arrows
point to a car-dotted patch,
the inventory of parts. Something will come
clear there, opines the retired tire king.

Maps, clues, knishes and I'm on my way,
clutching their map of my destiny,
the illegible commentary, the ornate
symbols like a zoological graph of my soul.

At the squashed hedgehog I know
to turn right. I cross tracks
with stalled trains in the distance,
loading and unloading.

A generation of architects wave t-squares
from the clouds. Cousin Bernie wants me to hurry,
"because we're hungry." But I get lost.
I'm gone a long time.

# Winter Storm Survival Guide

Call the snow a drunken sailor.
Ask why it's so afraid of sky
it runs away with all its baby white
bit-of-cloud belongings, sucking its thumb.

Listen for answers in freedom's bell,
which only mimics the sound
of an ancient contract tearing.

Find a passage that mirrors
the World's Fair's tallest slide
which you didn't dare and after
you finally did, you wouldn't go home.

Think the ground must be refuge
in an anti-angelic calculation.
Call the snow your ghost.

Carry your little crusts of paradise
as far as you can fly.
Get thoroughly sick of them. Keep falling.
You don't yet know what the hunger will be.

# Smut Creek

This is the creek which has always collected itself.
These are the fibrous bits of thistle.
Nobody fishes here.

That cluster of rushes looks like a genius,
messy hair, bright ideas
shooting off in every direction,

I know exactly what I must do
to be happy. But I can't be bothered.

Tangle of root, cement slab,
oak heaving up
through old foundations.

Ants crawl over slime traced with patterns
of more soggy stems, matted leaves.
I have let this happen.

Creek bed, teach me not to fear tick or snake,
but to watch the water bug with perfect love.
Let me stay here till a busload of biologists

clambers through, numbering me
with the stinging, the succulent,
the creatures who need no forgiveness.

# Limitations

*Our limitations are our gateways to reality*
          —Flannery O'Connor

Skin, nails, hair. If dropped from a height, this body breaks.
If opened, bleeds. If walked too far, thirsts,
tires, and yes, whines: weeping and complaining:

Of such there is no limit.
Top shelves, always out of reach, always contain a prize.
On sunny days, my shadow refuses to leave me.

Inside my body, like nesting dolls, the shriveled bodies
of Mother and Grandma crouch, stripped of cancerous organs.
Once, in another century, those parts provided food and shelter.

Meanwhile, mouth chews and swallows,
chews and swallows, interrupting ethereal pursuits.
Aided by gestures, this same mouth and tongue prays.

The God for whom I have taken up pen
speaks too quietly for my ears
to tell words from river hum.

Nearby is a gateway of splintered,
weathered wood, separating field
from field. Cattle gaze at it, then look back

to their work: grass chewed to manure.
My hands could open the gate.
Keeping them in my pockets,

I walk beside the fence.

# Sticky Truth

Sap buckets are up again,
clinging to maple bark
the way Doc Harlow's monkey
hugged its dry-teated carpet mother

because (as the experiment proved)
we all need to cleave
to something soft
whatever it secretes.

Despite their yearly extractions,
these maples keep growing.
Me, I had to stop some years ago.
Wind blows through my veins.

In another, more solid life,
I pour sap into a vat,
keep the fire lit and stir,
trusting gravity enough

to believe that the buckets
are filling nicely, each warming degree
shaking sap's flow loose
without even trying to be metaphorical.

Seekers after sweetness, are we
any more than tree
and bee parasites,
worshipping what feeds us?

# Calling Small Songbirds

I'm having the climbing dreams again.
Sometimes boulders gather, block my ascent.
If they were to let loose, I'd be crushed.
Nevertheless, my hands seek their narrow cracks
and ledges. I climb with difficulty, Mother's fears
for safety hovering behind my left ear.

Claws hold sideways to an arrow of ice
while I conjure names: sparrow, black capped chickadee,
thrush. As the day warms, icicles plunge
near feeding birds. The titmouse in his curlicue flight
thrusts up and down against air like a swimmer.

The cats start out of repose into perfect attention,
heads uptilted in that ancient posture of praise,
another name for desire.
Prisoners of the belly, we long to be fed
with something that thrashes. Titmouse looks around,
sees through the glass and his song turns sharp.

# Greylock

Midway up this, the tallest hill for miles,
I almost don't notice the imposters
hidden among birch and oak, cloaked in vines and mist.

Like the others, they grow towards the sun
but I see their brown trunks are metal, rusting
beneath peeling green paint on some,
red paint on others.

Relics of abandoned ski lifts emerge suddenly,
giant skeletons, trapped in time.
I see my childhood flit among them,
part of the distant past when these ruins
were erected fresh from the foundry.

I hope to follow their example
and merge back into forest,
releasing all ambitions, dreams of swift ascent.

# Towering Graveyard

Released by sun from their shining isolation,
the icicles outside my window keep slipping.

It's a shotgun wedding—
They're forced into melting embrace

as they hit the ground.
Merged, they freeze again.

Rocks take millennia to become this resigned
to rounded edges, blunted ambition,

till they end up like herds
of extinct earth eaters

all stunned into immobility,
as am I, by the uninterpretable

smile of a prophet, his misty
gaze falling like rain on the page,

blurring torrents of story
into one unpronounceable name.

# Inheritance

Always a sweater handy in that world,
my mother's world, now mine.

The globe's tossed, though
we were never much at catch,

daydreamers in the outfield,
getting famous bloody noses.

Sweaters come on and off,
raising and lowering like tides,

bodies too warm, too cold,
an endless retelling of brown-haired goldilocks

where nothing is ever "just right"
except in soundest sleep.

# Dreaming of Here

I

Yes, it's that apocalypse, the one where you grab
for rubble from the block where you grew up,
hoping letters from the "Frank's Sweet Shop"
sign resolve to spell "this way back."

(To note even parenthetically
that the dirt road swirls
under your feet is to risk the obvious,
but I'll say it anyway.)

The usual motion of the earth distorts,
some angel's running fingers
on a wet wine glass rim, hitting the note
that starts to rupture the planet

and you're trying to find a solid place,
not easy on a surface of a thousand sinewy branches.
You don't want to be the homesick kid
wiping her eyes whenever a counselor nears but

there's bigger battles: Here's the mutant
orthodontist who wields his sister's flaming baton.
Sweetie, rah rah mantras claim too many lives.
This parade marches to the landfill and composts.

II

White clad figures, gloved and goggled,
instruct us about the destiny
of our toxins, our future spread
out like so many sacrifices

34

God had the foresight to forsake,
repudiating them for finer details:
mosquito wings and tail fins
from rusting Chevrolets.


III


Turtle doves coo softly
on their altar—the fire escape.
Below, whores beckon and call
their mournful feathers away

In our separate beds, we batter
against the loneliness, reading
prophecies in the scattering
of torn pillow feathers

and giving thanks for the collisions
that didn't occur: dangerous
intrusions, like intersections
of crazy curving streets,

paved long after bears made
the first tracks, deciding
what *here* meant and where *there* would be.
*There,* now, is the town dump,

its maw the gate, the crimson gate.

# Hunger Stones

Travelling for the usual recreational purposes,
we stumbled upon warnings: words
carved on stones, revealed by drought.

Those who had scratched them praying
that only fishes who couldn't read
would see the marks yet knowing we would come

to study the runes as if they could help us understand
our fate, imagining us, hating us, because we had not yet suffered
as they had but they knew we would, we were stupid

some of us would scoff, bring spray paint, scrawl see, we are here,
and if not we, then someone else in five centuries will be here
and read our words, our graffiti, our tweets, our poems

they will wear gas masks or space suits
they will conjure water out of molecules
make it rain from blasted asteroids.

we will not weep we will not weep.

# Hammering in the Walls

Here on East Fifteenth Street,
no one mentions the hammering
which proceeds night and day:

renovation perhaps
or the universe dismantling itself,
insisting upon its own rhythm.

Here in my apartment, in my rocking
chair, my pulse slows then skips,
trying to synchronize

with the brittle heartbeat of hammers
for which steel beams make
perfect transmitters.

I'm forced to leave my cat and creep
in search of this tormenter, down a carpeted hallway,
eerily unlike my own despite its being identical:

different hums emanate from behind the same
doors, a welcome mat is missing from D,
cancerous Indian corn dangles from F

where it has never hung; until
I arrive at J, my own letter, J for joint, J
for jilted Jenny, J for Jesus, acquainted with hammers.

I arrive at the apartment just above mine,
and bending down, peer through the inevitable
hole from which a lock has been removed,

implying, as I quickly confirm, that this J
is vacant. A blue slot for the air conditioner
sucks chill gusts through to my eye.

The hall plays at stillness, no shake of life
or recent tumult. No one is here.
No one hammers.

Careful of this silence, I tip toe home,
sink into my white rocker and listen to it start again,
blow after echoing blow.

The hand behind the hammer
hesitates
for just a second.

I can do nothing in the small space
between reverberation and impact, but throb:
balloon into the pain.

J, I remember now, is for Job's
first replacement daughter Jemimah
who, overhearing God deal

with the old man, hovered
suspended above the city in a room
like this, urgently secure,

a room
where the hammering always threatens,
where I'll spend slow

shocked hours watching
a maneuvering of sky from blue
to bluer blue, to bluest,

as if it were a vision of progress.

# Dream Waste

We sing through our diminishments

diminuendo, decrescendo
croak to whisper

Rainbows split off

monochromatic snakes
slithering to black

# All is All

You're such a pest
nudging me with wet nose
though it is I who am your pet
who must grow tame

and learn to curl up at your roots
lick your talons
perform feats
of submission to gravity

O reality your deep silence
your playful chatter
your damaged children
and their thundering angels

sleeping monsters and waking dreams
branching dirt trails and fierce
glimmering freeways swept by sirens

trickles and floods
candle flame lightning bolt stroke
All is all now or never forever

# Ghostly Rider

Breathing bus fumes, gazing
deep into bulletproof glass,
I see myself,

one more coated commuter
filing onto the five fifteen
that slips through tunnel, pressing river out

till the city juts up beside us, spires orange
with Jersey haze. Condominiums rise
from meadowlands where

a great blue heron,
cold and filling the sky,
soared on wings like smoke.

I might have dreamed it.
At the toll gate,
the bus driver pays for us all,

and we turn off onto town roads.
Passengers pull the buzzer,
lurch forward, spill out to houses

tucked in quarter acres,
each one clutching a story
no one tells.

One held mine in a house
circled by rose bushes and,
half a hundred years later,

I step again off the bus that groans
as camels do
when they kneel and rise.

# Vagabond on the Fourth of July

The center isn't everything,
you announce by walking
away, the only direction.
Maps have so many arrows radiating
you trash them all and trample
over the single distance, out past
the winnowing fault, where cattle
study your worn boots and farmers
wonder what's out by the fence.
Is it so strange to refuse help
when help approaches drooling?
Reject the particular and walk.
It's still summer. Your tent
contains a special little solitude
that muffles the explosions
of patriotism all around,
the occasional hand
sent sailing to the sky.
Soon winter will
worship at the flap
and lead a private pilgrimage
to horseshoe heaven
where all your almosts count,
where the empty strip
your life has swathed
blackens the night sky.
You are the meteor that erases.

# About the Author

Robin Amelia Morris worked in film and video post-production in New York City before she moved to the hills of Western Massachusetts. There, she earned a Master of Fine Arts in Poetry as well as a Doctorate and now teaches online. Her poems appear in various journals, such as *The Comstock Review, Windhover, Blueline, American Literary Review,* and *The Lowell Review.*